Don't Call Me Turtle

BY
Elaine A. Powers

ILLUSTRATIONS BY
Nicholas Thorpe

Don't Call Me Turtle!
By Elaine A. Powers

Copyright © 2015 by Elaine A. Powers.
All rights reserved.
ISBN-13: 978-1517509576
ISBN-10: 1517509572

Published by Lyric Power Publishing LLC, Tucson AZ 2015

No part of this publication may be reproduced or retransmitted in any form or by any means, including, but not limited to, electronic, mechanical, photocopying, recording, or any information storage or retrieval system, without prior written permission of the publisher or copyright holder. Unauthorized copying may subject violators to criminal penalties, as well as liability for substanial monetary damages, costs, and attorney's fees.

All information provided is believed and intended to be reliable, but accuracy cannot be guaranteed by the author or the publisher.

My name is Myrtle. I'm a tortoise, not a turtle.
Being properly identified is my biggest hurdle.
Correct names are important, I'm sure you'll agree.
Let's look at the differences, they're easy to see.

Some turtles swim and some live in the sea,
But that's a place tortoises never should be.
Don't throw in the water a tortoise you've found.
You wouldn't be helping, in fact he would drown.

Our feet provide a simple clue
In the way they're shaped and what they do.
Turtles need water, so have webs between their toes,
Stout legs like elephants' take us tortoises where we goes.

Now check out my nails, another difference you'll see,
Caused by my preference for land over sea.
Turtles' nails are long and sharp, even longer in hims,
I like digging, not swimming, so keep my nails neat and trim.

Not all turtles swim like my friend they call a Box.
His shell closes with hinges, so he won't be eaten by a fox.
We all have round shells that we hold on our backs,
They give us protection in case we're attacked.

My tortoise shell is heavy, it takes strength to walk on ground.
But a turtle's shell is lightweight, perfect for swimming around.
Where tortoises have high domes, a turtle's shell is sleek
To go swiftly through the water—look down, take a peek!

The dome of the box turtle is the exception to the rule,
It's high like a tortoise's, isn't that cool?
Even though we're all called hard-shells, some turtles are soft as leather.
Whether hard or soft, our shells protect us from predators and weather.

Tortoises, turtles, too, have skeletons, inside and out,
These structures are required for moving us about.
The top is called the carapace, the plastron's underneath,
The bridge connects the two of them to make the shell complete.

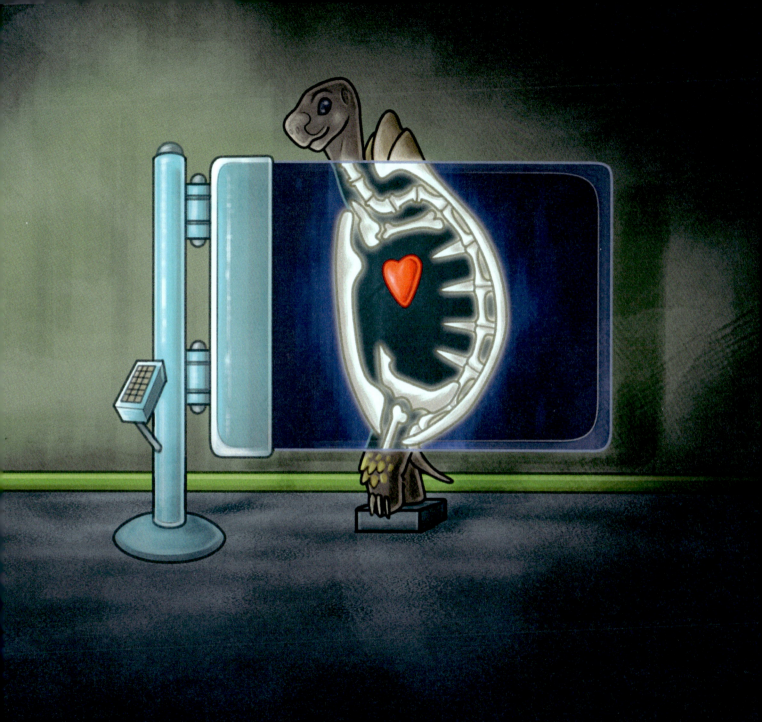

Scutes made of keratin provide the covering skin.
Turtles shed their scutes to grow, tortoises just add more keratin.

Nature gave hard-shells their own natural beauty,
Keeping them clean and unadorned is everyone's duty.

Don't add paint or polish, no extra color is needed.
These stop our shells from growing, this warning must be heeded.

Look deep into our eyes,
another difference looks back,

Turtles have colored irises
while tortoises' are black.

Desert tortoises are different, their irises are white.

A special adaptation for living in bright light.

Both turtles and tortoises on carrion like to snack,
But if tortoises eat too much, we get bumps upon our backs.
Turtles like their meat with veggies on the side,
Tortoises prefer the grasses, in which we also hide.

All hard-shells are reptiles, we have scales and breathe the air.
We all lay eggs on land but not just anywhere.
Females choose the perfect place, deep within the ground,
The eggs develop in the nest without their Moms around.

Ah, the noble tortoise, found in many lands.
From deserts to rainforests, we find life grand.
Tortoises can be big or small, and go about by day,
And tortoises are shy, wishing others would stay away.

A group of tortoises is called a "creep,"
We like walking on land that isn't too steep.
Our pace is slow but that's okay;
We have many years to find our way.

Turtles and tortoises are all unique and all deserve respect.
We hard-shells can only exist by sticking out their necks.

I hope my words have proven we are not all the same,
And when you see a tortoise, you'll use the proper name.

Next time you see someone like me
Use the clues to make your ID.
We can eliminate my biggest hurdle.
If together we shout:

"Please, Don't Call Me Turtle!"

Acknowledgement:

I'm grateful to those who helped me with this book: for their critical reading and suggestions from Pamela Bickell, Marilyn Buehrer, Brad Peterson, Kate Steele, Elise Stone, and Jill Jollay; my editors Annie Maier and Nora Miller; and, most importantly, to my reptilian inspirations: Myrtle "I'm not a turtle" Red-Foot Tortoise and Trevor Box Turtle.

Made in the USA
San Bernardino, CA
02 April 2016